Winging FREE

A VOLUME OF EXPERIMENTAL POETRY

DREW SLATER

WINGING FREE
A VOLUME OF EXPERIMENTAL POETRY

iUniverse books may be ordered through booksellers or by contacting:

iUniverse
1663 Liberty Drive
Bloomington, IN 47403
www.iuniverse.com
1-800-Authors (1-800-288-4677)

Because of the dynamic nature of the Internet, any web addresses or links contained in this book may have changed since publication and may no longer be valid. The views expressed in this work are solely those of the author and do not necessarily reflect the views of the publisher, and the publisher hereby disclaims any responsibility for them.

Any people depicted in stock imagery provided by Getty Images are models,
and such images are being used for illustrative purposes only.
Certain stock imagery © Getty Images.

ISBN: 978-1-5320-6878-2 (sc)
ISBN: 978-1-5320-6879-9 (e)

Library of Congress Control Number: 2019901858

Print information available on the last page.

iUniverse rev. date: 04/15/2019

A New Start

Hurry! Hurry! The last train is leaving
It's blowing its whistle. There's no time for grieving
You've a new tie to wear. And a new tie to form
A new face to wear. Never mind what you've worn
It's time for hearing drummers! Of that you're mighty proud
You don't know your calling, but the beat is mighty loud
Follow your own hoofbeats. They are all who know
Where it is you've been, and where you've got to go

Writers' Workshop

Twelve writers gather today
To tell you we are more than just a name
Each one with something to say
That no one else will ever say the same
Each one with something to show
Some nuggets made of phrases he has mined
Each one with somewhere to go
A Destiny that only he can find

Family

Oh, I've a family living in this land
There're five of them I try to understand
A sunny dad, a luminous mother
A pretty girl, a pair of fiery brothers
Oh, how I wish my family got along!
They will if they can keep from doing wrong

Oh, I've a family living on this earth
A Brotherhood of Man that's seeking birth
There're sunny dads and luminous mothers
And pretty girls and cannon-firing brothers
Oh, how I wish my family got along!
We will if we can keep from doing wrong

Oh, I've a family living in my soul
There're ten of them, and they are getting old
A sunny dad, a luminous mother
A pretty lamp and seven fiery others
Oh, how I wish my family got along!
They will if I can keep from doing wrong

Unplayed Music

Under my own skin
There's a violin
That I find so hard to play
All my deepest woes
Stradivari knows
But in words no tongue can say

All the long good-byes
Are a song that cries
In a voice that strikes no ear
All the lonely ends
Are my only friends
The rest is gone; they're here

In the cool of night
I see jewels bright
And the eyes of phantom birds
If I try one string
On my violin
Will my silent song be heard?

 Moonlit Rapture

The evening's full of promises and moonbeams unbended
I'm waiting for a splendor-girl that's heavenly to see
The stars are all aglitter, like snowflakes suspended
I'm waiting for a tender bird to do a song for me
    So bring it to me now
    And sing it to me now
    And fling it to me now
      I need
      A thing of beauty now
      That is what moonbeams are for
    There's haze in what I feel
    And blaze in what I feel
    And daze in what I feel
      Silvery
      Rays in what I feel
      That is what moondreams are for

There's magic in the murmurings of leaves that are blowing
She's waiting in the clearing now amid the winds and rain
I flounder in a whirling web she weaves without knowing
I'm waiting for a hearing now and for a sweet refrain
    So play it for me now
    And say it for me now
    Display it for me now
      Won't you
      Okay it for me now
      That is what night's glow is for
    There's dew in what I feel
    And blue in what I feel
    No clue in what I feel
      There's only
      You in what I feel
      That is what night's show is for

One of Those Days

A fly is in my ear buzz-buzz
Eight wheels screech I hate this heat
They say she maddens me she does
I should've turned on Davis Street
My throat's a-fire my eyes are glass
Is this my lane oh where's that map
My doctor's going to Spain alas
That mugger was a frightful chap
My keys are gone I left them home
The office isn't on this floor
Deliver me O Saint Jerome
I thought I paid that bill before
I touch the nearest lamp I'm shocked
What do I owe it's six percent
The frij is broke the toilet's blocked
I might as well just pitch a tent
The hall is jammed the noise the smoke
They're talking at me "yeah" he said
I think she laughed was that a joke
Will chaos only spare the dead
I'm dropping change what is the fare
My valiant team again was trounced
It's overcooked I asked for rare
Our records show your check has bounced

A Place Not Fondly Remembered

What was Dizzyland?
The circus? An amusement park?
There was no admission charge
But you paid to get out
There were no smiles at Dizzyland
No Ferris wheels
But many a merry-go-round
With only sad-faced clowns to ride them
The puppet show never ended
Joy on those premises strictly forbidden

There were animals and birds
Of every size and color
All beautiful, all neurotic
There were tightropes a-plenty
Quicksand safety nets
A jagged roller-coaster ride
You boarded at your peril
The Tunnel of Love was the exit
It wasn't easy
Growing up in Dizzyland

Phases

Wife, I can't believe our child!
Lately she has grown so wild
Weeks ago she was meek and mild
But husband dear,
It's just a phase she's going through

Mommy! Mommy! Come and sit
Look at how the moon is lit!
Weeks ago she was just a slit
But daughter dear,
It's just a phase she's going through

Oh, there'll be times when your soul will shine!
And there'll be times when all is dark
Times to glow
And times to be a dormant star

Separate Voyages

Child of the sea
You were born to sail the morning free
Sad melody
Do not fear you've left a tear with me
You've got dreams for finding
The captain of your ship must be your heart
And the streams are winding
And you will enter ports you must depart

Sail now, and find
Even though you've got to go, you'll cry
Don't look behind
For the stern's no place to learn good-bye
Sound the drum, O drummer!
For I have also streams that I must roam
Will there come some summer
When I will find some shore to call my home

Labels

Call me a winner, and see how I try
Call me a loser, and see how I cry
Call me important, and see how I glow
Call me invisible, and see how I go
Call me attractive, and see how I primp
Call me ungainly, and see how I limp
Call me a clown, and see how I grin
Call me a devil, and see how I sin
Call me superior, and see how I spurn
Call me inferior, and see how I burn
Call me a market, and see how I buy
Call me a soldier, and see how I die

Colors of Love

When love awakes the morning's gold
And every color's bright and bold
We're soaking up the sun we get
So certain it will never set
Till seeing red and feeling blue
And turning green are all we do
Mix them all, and mourning's black
And it won't give you golden back

A Dark Soul

"I've chased another drummer
A rose of summer
A rosy bummer!
I can't forget the cruelty
And how she fooled me
Yet still she rules me

I've got to find an answer
To lose this cancer
To join the dancers."
Even on the edge of hatred
There's something sacred
That helps you make it.

We don't claim all will heal, child of Scorpio
But to live is to feel; that, son, is all we know
Light is a spotless zero
That life has never been to
Dark, you're a seasoned hero
Every color's in you

Meteor on the descendant
We're all dependent
Upon that remnant
Of Spirit each man is blessed with
To build his nest with
And finally rest with

You've got to keep on going
That river's flowing
You can't be slowing
Phoenix upon the embers
Please help November
To not remember

All around you are fountains: laughers and weepers
But when pressures are mounting, still water's deeper
Light is a flashy zero
That love has never been to
Dark, you're the quiet hero
All your color's in you

My Father

His mind was young; his eyes were old
His heart was made of pure gold
For everyone became his child
And silver whiskers fringed his smile
He gave to everyone he knew
And jolly was his laughter too
The color he preferred was red
We looked at Dad and might have said
Santa lives

At eighty-past, he went away
To where it's Christmas every day
For there's no church where he had been
As mammoth as his own, within
And soon, it's Christmas once again
I'll see the kindly, red-robed men
Dispensing gifts and ambling slow
And I'll remember Dad, and know
Santa lives

The Gambler and The Maiden

O gambler, you who play the field
Behold a filly who might yield
A profit today
For you have kept a careful book
On all the figures worth a look
Her form is okay

A classy filly might prefer
To have a skillful jock on her
One who ain't hay
But she's been never really claimed
And she's been never really tamed
You're hoping she'll stay

She's wearing blinders more and more
And roses she's been longing for
A fire's within her
She knows her way without a map
Her weight is not a handicap
She might pay your dinner

You wonder: if you make a play
Will her reaction be a neigh?
She's still a beginner
But if that filly doesn't bolt
And doesn't quit beside a colt
You could be a winner

The Prosperous Pair

O Mortimer, you like mammoth fruits and vegetables in your field
So Hillary buys some fertilizer that will improve the yield
And Mortimer does the seeding, and Hillary does the weeding
Together they're a prosp'rous pair
Quite sure they won't be needing

Now Joseph piled up food a while, so later he could relax
And Mortimer saved up all his pay, and Hillary knew the tax
And Mortimer held the purse strings, and Hillary reimbursed things
Together they're a prosp'rous pair
Insured against adverse springs

When Mortimer buys he keeps his eyes on how much it all will cost
And Hillary knows the things she throws away are happily lost
But don't make your possessions a greedy-eyed obsession!
For where is there a prosp'rous pair
In Heaven's whole procession?

The Stranger

There's a stranger sitting on my shelf
And he looks as if he's filled with woe
Who is he? I often ask myself
Is he someone that I used to know?
Yes, I think that he is someone real
And I think I know who he might be
But he doesn't reveal
He stays quiet ... just like me

Hey, Stranger, don't melt away
We will meet again some day
Hey, Stranger, don't you cry
Even though we said good-bye
There's a time for rearranging
All the faces in my mirror
Some day, Stranger,
Yours will appear

Heavenward Gaze

O
Silver star above me
You
Are the only one I love
Oh,
Shine your kindness through me
Yours
Is the only glow that's true
With all my firefly friends gone
It's you that I depend on
O
Silver star, my heart's with you

O
Chains that held me gently
It's
Time to say good-bye again
Soft,
Flickering torch of freedom
You'll
Light the way that's right for me
O Heaven, you're my timepiece
And you will help me find peace
O
Stardust, I have trust in thee

O
Silver comet gliding
I
Crave your magic carpet ride
Fly
Me across that Jordan
Straight
To the love I've waited for
It's one-way passage only
Your flight need not be lonely
I'll
Be your friend forever more

The Winter Draft

When the winter strips the branches bare
The young and the green
Shall fall away
Die without a trace

He that plans the gardens doesn't care
If they won't be seen
Annuals, they
Easy to replace

They stood in parallel rows
Like pallbearers, mum
At their own funeral service
Young men waiting to be told
If they were healthy enough
For the grave

And as the death tolls rose
One more serf would come
Trying hard not to look nervous
They all knew he had no gold
If you were wealthy enough
You were saved

Hell, no – we won't go!
They would later be saying
More in anger than fright
But not he

Back then, he didn't know
After years of obeying
That he might have a right
To be free

When The Music Plays

Oh, there are times
When fences all around me loom
And make me feel I have no room
But when the music plays
It lets me travel far and wide
And visit places deep inside
That I no longer have to hide

Oh, there are times
When sorrows seem to have no end
And blackness is my only friend
But when the music plays
It comforts me and takes my part
It counts the beatings of my heart
It spurs me on; it helps me start

Oh, there are times
When I am standing so alone
Believing nothing that's unknown
But when the music plays
It tells me I must have a soul
A destination and a goal
A bonding that will make me whole

The Heart Queen

Her beauty is her lasting fame
Regard her high in any game
She's the Queen of Hearts
To top her, you must be an Ace
Or else the King of fairest face
Her counterpart
She's used to winning every trick
So if you ruff her, smooth her quick
Or you'll be foiled
Tumble a heart, and it's a spade
For love's a game not often played
According to Hoyle

My Brother

We played together from the start
We followed sports and studied art
He had a kind and gentle heart
My brother was my friend

The years went by and tall he grew
Computers were the thing he knew
But there was nothing he couldn't do
And nothing he wouldn't lend

The wheel all too quickly turned
Perhaps because rewards he'd earned
I couldn't believe it when I learned
His life had reached an end

My brother doesn't look behind
For he has gone to somewhere fine
From Mount Rainier, atop the snow
He gazes where the pine trees grow
At beauty only he can know

Green Entrapments

Green are the houses men design
So fragile seedlings will not wilt
Green is the hue of a bloomless vine
That hugs a fence that fear has built
Green are the pastures whose veneers
Beyond the fence have vexed it so
Green are the eyes that shed the tears
That watered the grass and made it grow

The Tennis Ball

Oh, take me out to the tennis courts
For I am a tennis ball
Pound and flail me all you want
And I'll keep bouncing tall
I'll know love means nothing
I will avoid the net
I'll keep bouncing far and free
And playing hard to get

To win you must have a racket
And a style deft and sly
At times you softly stroke at me
Then kiss that baby good-bye
Oh, show me where they play tennis!
It's the place where I belong
Where love means you got nothing
And good-bye isn't wrong

None But The Lonely Heart

Autumn haze and balmy days
Are gone so soon
The only pumpkin left was my coach

Winds so cool, winds so cruel
Now raid my tree
Of every friendly leaf that's shade to me
The birds of April go
Fair weather friends, they
Soon all that sings a song
And all that wings along
And all the colors Autumn brings are gone
So long .... So long ...

Jaunty styles and friendly smiles
No more to see
No welcome mat left at the door for me
I rap upon the wood
Nobody answers
None but the lonely heart
None but a homely heart
Could live to see his only home depart
While he's ... still there ...

Merging lines, converging lines
Far down the trail
A waving hand is slowly shrinking
Tiny ...
Tinier ...
And gone

Abandoned

Sometimes my rainbow's colors all turn to gray
Sometimes I wonder if God has gone away
I'll walk alone
Chilled to the bone
Tired of it all
How will I heed
If there's no call?

Faith is a gift, but sometimes it can be weak
When it's not strong, the future appears so bleak
How will I know
Which way to go
Which path is right
How will I see
If there's no light?

Our Collie

She was a dog of noble birth
And fully conscious of her worth!
For everyone Kim ever met
Agreed she was a gorgeous pet
You'd see her proudly prancing south
With some old shoe within her mouth
Or hauling branches twice her size
Determined to subdue her prize!
She'd growl and bark at passersby
But, left alone, she'd loudly cry
If she was chained she'd throw a fit
Till someone came to babysit
The family finally moved one year
And every eye held back a tear
For Kim was sent to "boarding school"
Where promptly she took up her rule!

Modern Art

Some people will hate it
Many will not understand
But the painter who makes modern art
Thinks it's beautiful
He ought to know
But some people shun what's different
Don't press the panic button!
It's just modern art

Some of God's children are born different
And different folks they will always be
But they are not worse
They're just modern art
Some people will hate them
Many will not understand
But the Artist who made them
Knows they're beautiful

The Quarterback

She puts her quarter in the phone
But will he ever be at home
Or call her back?

In football or in basketball
In love, or any task at all
He's quarterback

He'll fake and then complete a pass
Or he can score by being fast
For he's a rover

She gives that telephone a smack
But she won't get her quarter back
The game is over

My Place

It's not a castle or a treasure house
It's more a hassle than a pleasure house
The nearby traffic can produce a frightful din
I wish I had more space to put belongings in
But it's the place where I am free
The place where I am me
The place where I have been

The rent is higher than it used to be
And I'm more tired than I'd choose to be
The drafty winters are enough to make you freeze
The torrid summers leave you praying for a breeze
But it's the place that I know best
The place where I can rest
The place where I'm at ease

I wonder will I ever move away
Another building might improve the day
More ghastly neighbors you could never ever know
The evil landlord keeps on hoping I will go
But it's the place where I have stayed
The place where I have grayed
The place that I call Home

Liquid Lullaby

You are the water
Your motions melt and ripple as you walk
Your notions pour, legato, as you talk
In your oceans I am baptized
My emotions leave me capsized
Till the winds of time sweep me to a desert plain
Now I wander the burning sands, searching
Lurching from mirage to mirage
My arms thirst for the water that is you
You are my oasis
You are holy water in a lowly tavern
The only water for the lonely caverns of my heart
Pour your charms upon me like a waterfall of guile
And I will wring my raincloud eyes and smile

All I Need

You are my fortress
You are what makes me strong
You are my family
Telling me I belong
You are my light
When I feel lost and sad
You are my hope
When things look bad

You are my shelter
When I've been in the rain
You're my confessor
When I've been feeling pain
You are my nurse
Helping me when I bleed
You are my friend
You're all I need

Parenting

Theodore, O Theodore
You know every lass born
Needs a firmly moral dad
Like the one that you had
You will teach your kid the Law
Free her from her worst flaw
Then she will not bother us
That is how your father was

Emily, so sweet and mild
You know every last child
Needs a gentle, loving hand
Something she can understand
Love your kid with blindness
She'll respond with kindness
Just as any other does
That is how your mother was

Theodore and Emily
You both know the remedy!
Treat your daughter in between
Being lax and being mean
Can you learn to hear her?
She is not your mirror
Maybe stop and think a while:
Who's the parent? Who's the child?

A Free Soul

Doctor, Doctor
Put away thy stethoscope and laser beams
Lay aside your microscope, your healing teams
I am made of silver hope and golden dreams
You'll find my heart
Where the buntings fly
And in the blaze of sun, and in the pale of clouds
I'm winging free

Scholar, Scholar
Write me no biography, no rigid tome
Don't consult geography to find my home
Don't expect topography to fathom foam
You'll find my life
On an ocean wave
And in the phantom mist, and in the playful breeze
I'm winging free

Preacher, Preacher
Spare me all thy should-have-beens and sacred halls
Lead me not from all my sins and Adam's falls
I will follow footloose winds and cricket calls
You'll find my soul
Where the moonbeams dance
And in the glide of swans, and in the bound of deer
I'm winging free

The Rat Race Winner

The rat he runs a tricky maze
To win at every game he plays
For victory's the Swiss he chews
Too bad that others have to lose
Oh, why'd they say he had to win
Each crazy rat race he's been in?
For, though he cheats at games he plays
We know he did not make that maze

The Phonograph

Schubert records piled high
Chronicles of times you cried
Layers of a tortured soul
Anchored by an empty hole

Play your sorrow, treble high
Spin it like the turning sky
Needle's sharp, insistent dream
Cuts the grooves until they scream

Arm, you feel your way around
Toward rejection you are bound
Still you seek that empty core
Though you've heard that song before

Blue Oblivion

Neptune, love that I've long been chasing
Blue as the orbits I've been tracing
A moth was I
Now
I'd just like to glimpse you
To say good-bye

There were two that I thought might need me
There were two that I thought had freed me
Their eyes were blue
Soon
They'll shrug at my coffin
"What else is new?"

Raven, roving the sky forlornly
He is the only one who'll mourn me
He knows the blue
Wanderer
Feathered in ashes
I'll follow you

Tired from fleeing another scarecrow
You will fly to where they wouldn't dare go
Into the blue
There
Some sapphire's believing
My love was true

The Smile Seeker

Once there was a yellow-haired child
Dancing
In the snow of faraway Lapland
And she was happy

She lost her heart
To a man already wedded
To a muse that was embedded
In his Cellini-like hands

She lost her youth when she left her home
For a land she did not know
Beyond the Atlantic
And a man she did not know
Beyond the romantic
She needed something more to feel free

She lost her head
To the sweet red poison
Where all that's buoyant sinks
And all that's growing shrinks
She filled her glasses till they were rosy
And the world looked pretty again

She lost her child
In a court where charges flew
In a tongue she barely knew
The kid needed milk, not wine
She tried to take her bottle back
But there was no refund on what she had paid
And there was no future in being a maid

So back she went
Like so many others, lost and defeated
To the sweet red poison
Where they fill their glasses till they are dozing
And the mirrors look pretty again

But we know she must have tried
And we know she must have cried

She lost her legs
To the cruel white blood cells
She traveled on wheels
From bed to bed
From bad to worse
But she never lost her hope

She's gone now
To join the Source of her vitality and warmth
She's back in a land where the sun never sets

Perhaps I'll see her face some day
Or maybe a soul without a body
But whether she'll have legs or not
I know that she'll be dancing
And happy again

Kentucky Derby Post Parade

A Derby Day
Is a graduation day
Resplendent with sights and with sounds
The horses march
As the music starts to play
And the jocks wear colored caps and gowns

The "parents" watch
Feeling proud and yet concerned
You youngsters have gifts you must show
You're ready now
Every lesson has been learned
And today you all have far to go

Do the best you can now
Try not to come home late
At the rainbow's end
There are roses to be worn
It is time to tell the world
You are great

Anagram Life

Norma, your life like an anagram goes
For all that you see, you've got transposed
You think Tim's your teacher, but he can be a cheater
You think he's an angel, but he's got an angle
You think you're his teammate; he thinks you are tame meat

Better look again, Norma!
Are you his salve or his slave?
Is there a garden of roses? Or a danger of sores
Is his Earth trine? Or his heart inert
Does he orbit with Virgo? Or rob it with vigor
Does his star lead in March? Or do rats deal in charm

Who is Tim?
A live god? Or a vile dog
The saint that smiles? Or the slime that stains
A friend of many uses? Or a fiend of many ruses
A priest, whose caring words will serve you?
Or a spiter, whose racing sword will sever you!

Norma, your life, as you've known it, goes
When all you've been seeing gets exposed
Norma, our True Believer:
Live true, or a mourner be

Winter Angel

The snowy hills are desolate
The skies are gray with sorrow
You've gone to climb another mile
You've packed away my summer smile
O Angel of the highest hill
Will you be mine tomorrow?

There's frost upon the hourglass
The sand is sinking, way low
But when you're near, I'm young again
And I can feel the sun again
O Angel of the highest hill
Are Saturn's rings your halo?

A Politician Speaks

My fellow Americans:
We are today faced
Both at home and abroad
With escalating megalumphosis of the dollar
Coupled with the percalipgation of our gold supply
Upon which hinges the future of our Republic
I have therefore asked the legislature
For a ninety trillion dollar goblivogancy
On interest rates during the current fiscal year
Together with a six percent thermopolization
Over the next five years
These measures will effectively mobilize
Our phimalditudinal capacity
To a level approaching parity with the Japanese yen

It is truth that lights the eternal candle of God
So let me make this perfectly clear:
Some of you have inquired about the disgraced
Senator Grafton
The truth is, I did have a conversation with him
But what was discussed at the meeting, I cannot recall
I knew nothing of his alleged misconduct at that point
It goes against everything I believe in
I believe in America. I believe in the family
I believe that this nation under God
Has a destiny barely glimpsed thus far
The strength of our great land lies in its people
And in the values that our nation holds sacred
With God's help - -
And yours in November - -
We can and will restore to its full flowering
The glory and greatness of America
Thank you. God bless you
And God bless America

The Pulpit

Miss Pepper Piper papered
The Pope's pulpit purple
Now it's a palpably
Purple papal pulpit
And the Pope's purple
As the papering
Pepper Piper perpetrated!

Nunsense Rhymes

Sister D. I'll forever see
For within my brain she's seared!
A principal so invincible
That her every glare was feared
She would loom in the back of the room
Like a ghost you never heard
Then she'd drum you upon your thumb
With a ruler if you'd erred

Sister Mark never had to bark
Her hiss was worse than her bite!
She'd recoil and slowly boil
As a pupil cringed in fright
She would rage if a turning page
Made the slightest rustling sound
She would seethe if you dared to breathe!
Oh, her wrath was much renowned

Sister Ruth, I can say in truth
Had a shriek that made you totter!
Shook the room like a sonic boom
But it only made her hotter
All that smoke-if she had a stroke
It would set the school on fire!
She could match a tomato patch
When her face was red with ire

Sister E. was a friend to me
And to every other child
She was fun and a jolly nun
And she had a cheerful smile
She could teach any kid in reach
From a scholar to a dope
She was plump as an elephant's rump
But you'd see her skipping rope

Sister A. had a wild way
And she drilled the kids like troops
Eyes ablaze, like Hitler's gaze
When she called us "nincompoops"
She would march "by the numbers," starched
As her uniform severe
She would scream till the windows steamed!
It was Halloween all year

Sister L. was as old as hell
And I'm not sure she could hear
Calling me inadvertently
By another's name all year
What a hag! Why, she nearly gagged
When in Lent a sweet I ate
She was cold as December snow
On a cemetery gate

Sister G. I could plainly see
Had a cruel, sadistic streak
She made threats till you paid your debts
To the missions every week
She impaled till a child wailed
Even parents were appalled
In my dream, if you hear me scream
She's the witch that I've recalled

Sister M. was a frightful femme
Not a child didn't abhor
There was one that she stepped upon
After throwing him to the floor!
She would burn if you couldn't learn
She'd berate you if you failed
If you cried 'cause you'd really tried
She would coldly send for a pail

Sister R. was the champ by far
When it came to bumping ceilings
She was tall as a canyon wall
(And that was while kneeling!)
She was kind and her halo shined
She observed the Golden Rule
It was swell that I didn't get hell
In my final year of school

Spirit of Christmas

Chapel steeple, reaching high
Happy people passing by
Mistletoe, above my door
What's that glow you've waited for?
Rank and file sing of Jesus
People smile, just to please us
There's a feeling in the air!
Bells are pealing. People care
Hark! The herald angels knew
Christ is there, inside of you

Somewhere To Go

Deep, darkest night
You leave me lost and lonely
Yet not afraid of the journey I make
O lantern light
I count on you to show me
The twists and turns on the path I must take
O city strong, with twelve gates of entry
There I belong, and I will make it through
Don't you despond
For beyond this world of sorrow
There's somewhere to go
And there's someone to know
There's somewhere fine
And there is something divine

Safe in Her Loving Arms

Weary am I, in search of a place
In Mary's heart, I'll find space
Moonbeams smile on orphans of night
Hold me close and I'll feel all right
Virgin, carry me homeward
Mary, carry me home

Wanderer lost, tear in your eye
You've a home in the sky
Don't you know we are all of us guests
Winging southward toward our nest
Virgin, carry me homeward
Mary, carry me home

Time

Time, restless time
    tick ... tick ...
Why must you run?
    tick ... tick...
Why must you zoom
    tick ...
Somewhere beyond the sun
    tick ... tick ...
Where it's still June
    tick ...
All the faces
All the places dear to me
    tick ...
Turned to flee, far too soon
    tick ...

Time, racing time
    tick ... tick ...
Olympic foe
    quick ... quick ...
Faster by far
    quick ...
Than any man can go
    tick ... tick ...
Who has a heart
    tick ...
No one's needings
No one's pleadings mean a thing
    tick ...
They're on wing, from the start
    flick!

Time, cruel time
    tick ... tick ...
The sternest judge
    tick ... tick ...
No farewell blues
    tick ...
Could ever make you budge
    brick ... brick ...
And yet you lose!
    click!

What we see we photograph
And what we hear's on phonograph
And what we are
We will forever be
    tick ... tick ...
Alive and free
    tick ...
Homeward we shall run
    tick ...
Joined together soon
    tick ... tick ...
Beyond some sun
    creek ... creek ...
Where it's still June
    tick ... tick ... tick ...

Printed in the United States
By Bookmasters